The BE T GREATEST Handbook

Master and Apply the 10 Jewels of Greatness

Ydrate "The Great" Nelson, M. Ed

The BE THE GREATEST Handbook

Copyright © 2022 by Ydrate Nelson & Associates LLC/ BE THE GREATEST Publishing.

All rights reserved. No part of this publication may be reproduced, distributed, or transmitted in any form or by any means, including photocopying, recording, or other electronic or mechanical methods, without the prior written permission of the publisher, except in the case of brief quotations embodied in critical reviews and specific other noncommercial uses permitted by copyright law.

For permission requests, write to the publisher, addressed "Attention: Permissions Coordinator," Ydrate Nelson/ BE THE GREATEST. Publishing

3101 N. Central Ave Suite 183 #760

Phoenix, Arizona 85004

Book Layout ©2022 Ydrate Creates Design/BTG Media

Book Cover Design by Ydrate Creates Design/ BTG Media

Book Editor ISBN 978-0-9860929-6-1

1st ed

I pray that you and your family are blessed with peace, love, joy, prosperity, abundance, and overflow. You deserve the Best, and I pray that you are forever on the path of mercy, grace, and love.
BE THE GREATEST.

Greatness Guide

Maximize this Program. vii
Your GREATNESS Partner: ix
BE THE GREATEST. U x
The State of BE xvi
Be Motivated 1
Be Attentive 16
Be Strategic 28
Be a Master Communicator 38
Be Trustworthy 48
Be Savvy 60
Be Compassionate 70
Be Creative 82
Be a Visionary 92
Be Bold 102
BE THE GREATEST Bonus Resources. 112
The Life Balance Wheel 113
Create Mantra Statements 120
Create a Vision Statement 123

The mission of **BE THE GREATEST. U (BTG)** is to leverage education, fashion, influence, and entertainment to inspire higher achievement, increase self-esteem and maximize personal Greatness.

BE THE GREATEST.

Disclaimer: The information in this book is for educational and communication purposes and should not be a substitute or a replacement for professional medical advice, counseling, or treatment.

Every effort has been made to ensure this book is as accurate and complete as possible. However, there may be some mistakes in typography and evolutions in the content; therefore, the content will be updated over time.

As the content is updated, you can scan the code below and enjoy the newest digital version with personal narrations from the author. Your time, effort, and support are Greatly appreciated. BE THE GREATEST.

Maximize this Program.

This handbook is an easy short read designed to guide you to BE THE GREATEST version of yourself through mastering ten core competencies. The ten jewels are very simple and give discovery questions and action items to help create a plan to bring out your best. This book can be scanned, but the actual value comes from doing the exercises and mapping out a plan for your life so you can BE THE GREATEST that you can Be.

For maximum impact, take a week to focus on each jewel. The following week, review the previous weeks and add the current week until all ten jewels have been mastered. The goal is to help create change, which takes time to master.

Life is constantly changing, so the answers you put now might not be the same a few months later. Keep reviewing, answering the questions, and taking advantage of the recommendations. Update your results as you evolve as a person. You can read to get the information, but the true transformation will come from taking action to do the work.

About the Author Ydrate Nelson, M. Ed

Ydrate is an author, speaker, and multi-talented entertainer with over 20 years of professional experience connecting with audiences across various platforms and genres, from the classroom as the "Teacher of The Year" to stages inspiring thousands. As the owner of Ydrate Nelson & Associates LLC, Ydrate specializes in Motivational Speaking, Educational Consulting, and Greatness Life Coaching.

Ydrate is the creator of BE THE GREATEST U, a curriculum-based lifestyle brand whose mission is to leverage education, fashion, influence, and entertainment to inspire higher achievement, increase self-esteem and maximize personal Greatness.

While battling stage 4 colon cancer, Ydrate was reminded that no matter the outcome, good, bad, or indifferent, motivation, and mindset play a role in the results of your day-to-day life. Ydrate is now on a mission to help others cultivate a motivated mindset for success and BE THE GREATEST version of themselves.

Your GREATNESS Partner:

I Promise to *"INSPIRE"* you to BE THE GREATEST you.

I Promise to help *"MOTIVATE"* you in never giving up when you are at a crossroads in making a choice coming from your heart.

I Promise to be *"COMPASSIONATE"* to your thoughts and feelings while you unlock and open new doors to your life's true happiness.

I Promise to *"RESPECT"* who you are as a person and to bring out only the best in you.

I Promise to *"VALIDATE"* you through each door you unlock and open along the way with words of encouragement.

I Promise to *"SUPPORT"* you during your journey into yourself while you achieve moments of enlightenment.

I Promise to *"HONOR"* your light from within those shines and make the world a better place with your presence.

But most of all, I Promise to *"BELIEVE"* in who you are as a person, as you find the greatness within.

BE THE GREATEST. U

I genuinely believe every person was created to be great. However, it has been estimated that the average person usually operates at less than 50% of their potential. Most people are not motivated enough to reach their full potential and BE THE GREATEST version of themselves. Too many of us settle and live up to mediocre standards instead of stretching ourselves to greater heights of achievement.

If we learn how to master and apply the right success tools, we increase our chances of success over the person we used to BE. Our most significant default is often our faulty thinking and lack of effort. We don't strive to BE THE GREATEST because we don't believe we are Great.

Many speakers and authors write books to motivate people to be better versions of themselves. Many fail to realize that no one person can truly inspire genuinely to BE THE GREATEST. Each person must choose to motivate themselves and do the work required to be Great. The actual results come from the ability to boost the self and harness the power of execution intrinsically.

When we learn to BE THE GREATEST, we take control of our ability to complete tasks consistently. We also see an increase in our potential and inspire others to reach the heights of Greatness. While it may be unrealistic for all of us to get 100% of our full potential, we can set the bar high enough so that even if we fall short, we will still be much closer. If we don't strive to BE THE GREATEST, we settle for mediocre or the bare minimum. If we fall short of that, we are far beneath the heights of Greatness; we were created to BE.

Working as a high school teacher, in different leadership roles, as a motivational speaker, and Life Coach for years has given me the pleasure of partnering with many great people. Many are looking for ways to reach their goals and achieve Greatness. Their desire for improvement has always been a source of inspiration. I took the time to look at what has been successful in my life and the life of other successful people. It has been stated that success leaves clues. I began the quest to quantify the precise principles, fundamental patterns, proven exercises, and tested action steps that lead to personal Greatness.

My journey led me to a few principles I now call the Jewels of Greatness. As I reviewed the process of getting where I am today, mastering the ten jewels of Greatness has been the foundation of my personal and professional success. I didn't initially know a specific name for the skills that helped me reach the next level; I just knew I could leverage skills to help me advance. At first, I thought it was a gifted talent that was unique to me in some way. I thought I was special. I later realized these jewels are principles that can be learned, taught, and mastered.

My goal to find the most effective way to quantify the skills leads me on a path of self-discovery. I evaluated over **20 years of professional experience** as a high school and adult educator, management/leadership roles, marketing associate, and financial recovery specialist in industries including education, professional services, and depository institutions. I found that each part was different, but I still found success by applying similar methods, principles, and skills.

Understanding that most people desire to BE THE GREATEST version of themselves but don't exactly know what that looks like or how to achieve this goal leads me to quantify specific skills into a teachable system to guide and measure the effectiveness of the actions taken.

Even though there are some universal principles we can all follow, we can only define Greatness based on our standards and actions. We can never BE THE GREATEST compared to or strive to be like someone else. We can never BE THE GREATEST without a goal and map or plan to accomplish it. Not having an idea of what your GREATNESS looks like while striving to BE your Best is like driving around and guessing which way to go. When you know where you want to go, you find the right map to correct you. If your focus is not on doing your Best, you will never reach the highs of personal Greatness.

I remember back to my first year as a high teacher. I was teaching science with an emergency teaching certification to fill a shortage in that subject area. My background and education were in business and adult education. Even though I was not a fan of teaching science, I needed to show up to the students. Once I committed to teaching, I declared to myself, BE THE GREATEST Science Teacher I could be. I didn't go to school to teach, and I didn't have any knowledge or experience in science. There were other more tenured people with the education and the experience all around me. I knew I could not BE THE GREATEST if I competed against them. The other teachers were not my competition but my allies to help me BE THE GREATEST.

My goal was to BE THE GREATEST Teacher I could BE and not use time competing that I could be using to improve. I had to work twice as hard to learn information other teachers had already mastered in the classroom. Even when other teachers were not rushing to my aid or too busy to assist me, I never made an excuse because it was about finding a way to get it done for the students. I never lost focus on becoming a better teacher for my students. I never thought of another teacher as my competition. I just focused on what I could do to get better each day. By the end of the first semester, my students were on par with all the district science classes; I even won my school's "Science Teacher of the Semester."

The key to my success was setting a goal and locking in on what my Greatness looked like each day. My focus was on me and my desire to BE THE GREATEST Teacher and no one else. I would see what the other teachers did and implement the best strategy for my students. I understood that my goal to BE THE GREATEST Teacher was not about me but about my students and the community I serve. Within three years three, I went from a part-time substitute to "Teacher of the Year" by committing to BE THE GREATEST Teacher in the classroom and applying the jewels of Greatness.

The question is, what do you want to be the Greatest at? Is it your job, marriage, parenting, or just to BE THE GREATEST? Make the declaration and go for it. BE THE GREATEST.

If you want to learn how to adopt and leverage the Jewels in your life to maximize Greatness the same way I did, this book is right for you.

Each chapter begins with a personal story followed by application recommendations and coaching questions.

Furthermore, readers will also learn they can apply the Jewels in their lives through easy methods.

Reflect on the questions below and continue to lay the foundation for your mindset of Greatness.

BE THE GREATEST U. BE THE GREATEST.

WHAT MAKES YOU GREAT?

HOW DO YOU DISPLAY YOUR GREATNESS DAILY?

HOW CAN YOUR BECOME GREATER?

WHAT DOES GREATNESS MEAN TO YOU?

The State of BE.

I had to accept the realization that I must become what I desire to be. We are all so busy with so many different things going on in our lives. When we look at all the things we must do, it is easy to get overwhelmed. When we reach this point, we are more likely to revert to what we have built ourselves to be via habit and lifestyle choices. For example, if you work on being a positive person daily, at some point, you will not have to think about being a positive person; you will become a positive person and live a positive life.

If you are used to being negative, your mind is more likely to see the situation negatively because that is who you BE when hard times hit. You can do many things, but it takes time and cultivation to become what you are based on what you do. Many people will give up before they reach a point of doing something habitually that becomes second nature. You do it without thinking because you have been programmed to feel that way. I had this example show up in my life significantly recently.

In June of 2021, I was diagnosed with stage 4 colon cancer.

The news was devastating because I had three small kids, and my wife was pregnant with our 4th child. Even though this was a rough time in my life, I still approached each day with the most positive attitude. My mind was accustomed to embracing high-vibrating thoughts and positive energy. Even on the worst days or scenarios, my brain was conditioned to think positively. At first, I had to work hard at thinking positively and looking on the bright side no matter what. Over a period, I no longer had to think about being positive or doing positive things. I became a positive person because of the actions I took each day. It became who I was and not just something I was doing.

No matter the obstacle, I always tried to find the positive or bright side, and the person I had become was a huge asset in my cancer battle. I considered my cancer diagnosis a blessing because it allowed me to show up as THE GREATEST version of myself and to stand fully in the positive light I had built myself to Be. I watched other people I know struggle through various illnesses and obstacles in their lives.

When they would make the brave attempt to change their life by changing their mindset, many people become exhausted. They had more stuff to do. More things to consider and add to a busy life and already full plate. When we get tired, worn down, and exhausted, we are more likely to return to our old habits or ways of thinking.

Therefore, we must embrace the state of BE. When we do, our habits guide our actions to the point that it is less likely that we will get overwhelmed or revert to activities we desire to avoid. Even though I was built for adversity mentally, this was not the case on all levels, and it showed up in my life during my cancer battle.

In my mind, I could stay positive most of the time, even when given less favorable news. This was all from habits I formed over a long period. I had become a person who cultivated a mindset to handle adversity with positivity. While I was firm in one area of whom I had become, I was exposed to my diet and lack of discipline. The theme was again echoed, it's not what you do but what you BE.

During my cancer battle, I was also diagnosed with prediabetes. I knew that a massive component of my negative diagnosis and my ability to prolong my life was based on my ability to make a lifestyle adjustment. I had to make vigorous diet changes to reverse some of the adverse effects of what was done. I was 5'7, 240 pounds, stage 4 cancer, and prediabetic. Even though my positive mindset development was significant, my diet and eating habits were terrible. I had to find a way to get my mindset around my diet to the level I had cultivated myself for positivity.

The cancer started in my colon and moved to my liver. After seeing people, I know personally, as well as celebrities, battle the same disease and have a variety of outcomes, I had to face reality. One day I was conversing with one of my naturopathic doctors about my mortality. I asked him what the more immediate threat to my life was. He let me know that it was not based on what was in my body now but on what I put in my body moving forward. Over the years, I formed many terrible eating habits that became my lifestyle. When I was hungry, I would eat whatever I wanted. Many times, whenever I wanted. I was good at managing life's adversities but poor at staying focused on my diet.

I was all in when it was time to embrace my new lifestyle. I went vegan after eating meat my entire life. I cut all sugar and found foods that were considered anti-cancer. I ate things that I had never heard of in my life. I abandoned all my traditional meals for a complete shift. It was a conscious daily grind. I focused on my diet, physical activity, and mental space. It was a new reality for me. I worked hard to figure out a strategy. Over a period, I was able to lose weight and reverse the diabetic diagnosis. At my best, I went from 240 down to 193. My goal weight was 185. It took a lot for me to create a plan to yield the results I wanted and needed for survival.

After going through an abbreviated chemotherapy process, an intense naturopathic approach, and surgery, that removed part of my liver, I worked my way from stage 4 to stage 0. I didn't have cancer, but I had cancer cells floating throughout my body. I decided not to take on more chemotherapy at the time following surgery. I knew I was taking a chance but felt I could keep cancer from returning with the proper diet, vitamins, and overall health regimen.

Over a few months after my surgery and stage 0 status, I found it harder to maintain the lifestyle I needed to keep cancer from posting up in my body. I worked out a bit less and ate unhealthy food a bit more. It was a gradual process happening a little bit at a time. Before I knew it, I was getting closer to my old habits. I knew it would take much focus to achieve my goal of beating cancer.

After a few months, I had to revisit the doctor for a checkup, on the same day that I was diagnosed with cancer the year prior, June 22. I had been traveling a bit and was off my program more than I should have been. I was still hopeful that I was good. I got my bloodwork and noticed my cancer marker had increased and my immune system was compromised. I could tell my body was fighting hard. After that, I had my first scan, and it looked like they found something, but I had more scans later in the day to confirm.

After my second scan, it was confirmed that they found more cancer in my body, and I was back to stage 4 again. I have been diagnosed with stage 4 cancer twice in one year. The next stage was for more scans to see how serious the situation was and see if the cancer was progressing. I knew if I beat cancer before, I could do it again, but it would not be easy. I took my moment to accept my reality before regrouping for war.

I decided to transfer my treatment to the cancer center in my home state of Georgia, where I have more family and friend support. My appointment was about a month after my last meeting, and I took that time to focus on my health. I started working out daily and eating healthy. I began to put vitamins and minerals in my body and cut off most of my unhealthy habits. I was locked in on my health and mental wellness.

When I went to my appointment in Atlanta a few weeks later, I received some of the best bloodwork I had ever had, and the cancer was not progressing. I was given various ways to address cancer in my body, and he left the choice up to me. I decided to create my treatment program based on the information I collected during my cancer battles.

Lesson learned

As I sat to strategize my next move, I knew that I was missing a lesson in my journey. There was no way I could go from stage 4 to stage 0 back to stage 4 and not learn something. It finally dawns on me. I found a series of activities that worked during my cancer battle and started to do these things consistently. I was eating healthy, working out daily, filling my body with vitamins, praying, meditating, and going to the doctor often to make the proper adjustments. Focusing on my health was a full-time job, but I was doing what I needed to do.

As I continued to do what I needed, I also had to take on my other life and family responsibilities, adding more things to my to-do list. The more I added to the list; the more things started to fall between the cracks. I was getting overwhelmed by all the things I had to do. I was doing too much.

Even though I was doing the best I could to do what needed to be done, I was still struggling. Over the year, I built myself to be motivated and cheerful, but I needed to become a new person. I needed to become a healthy person, not just someone who did healthy things. We are human beings, not humans having or doing things. However, we spend so much time doing stuff so we can have something that we become redefined by what we want and not who we are.

I learned that doing what needs to be done is not good enough; you need to transform and become the person you need to BE. So, at the end of the day, if I truly wanted to beat cancer, doing what needed to be done was not good enough. I had to become a new person. I had to change what I had become and form new habits aligned with the person I needed to beat cancer.

So, as you go through these jewels in this book, don't think about just doing what you need to do; think about the person you need to become to reach your most excellent version. You were created to be Great. Now BE THE GREATEST you can be. You deserve your best, and so does your family and the people you are called to serve.

> What do you Be? When you look at your habits and mindset, who have you become? Who have you cultivated yourself to

Your Quest to BE THE GREATEST Begins Now. Introducing The 10 Jewels of Greatness.

Be Motivated

My motivated mindset has been the foundation of most of my success. I recognized early on in life that to BE THE GREATEST, you must be motivated to reach your full potential. Without motivation, many of your goals and tasks will fall to the side. I learned to harness the power of motivation and have used it as my superpower for years. Each day I try to find a way to either create and spread motivation or embrace it from the many motivating factors in life.

My motivated mindset is not based on some fictitious world where everything is perfect and happy. It is based on the opposite. It is easy to quit and give up when things are hard. I try to find the motivation to get me back to the top. A primary key is always finding and focusing on your why or goal. What is the purpose? What is the driving force that makes me go?

I remember when I was in my 20s, and my car broke down. I was living in metro Atlanta, Georgia, and having a vehicle is vital to move around the city. I got a new job working at a collection agency not far from where I lived to make it easy to get to work. My motivation was to get a new car.

From the first day, I walked into the building; I was focused on making and saving enough money to get myself a car. I had to catch a ride to work each day. That meant I had to depend on other people to pick me up and drop me off. I was not too fond of it. I knew if I hit a certain number of accounts collected, I would earn not only my base salary plus commission on top. I went to work motivated every day with a mission to get what I wanted.

During the first month at the job, I was the rookie of the month and earned a parking space outside in the front of the building. The parking space had a reserved sign with the words "top performer" on it. They added my name to the slot under top performer. I had a prime-time parking slot with my name on it, and I didn't even have a car. Everyone who worked in this building would walk by this empty slot with my name on it.

At this point, I didn't have enough to get the car I was working for. I had to continue to come to work and keep pushing. I was motivated by seeing that empty slot with my name on it. I would let my friends park there, but I wanted my car parked there.

The following month, I was the top performer again and

getting closer to reaching my financial goal. My name remained on the spot designated for the top performer right in front of the building. I was humbled each day as I walked by that slot with my name on it. As people would pull into the parking lot and scramble for a place to park, I had a primetime slot with no car. I used that as motivation to drive me to become a top performer. With that effort, I finally got the car I wanted, a white Lexus. At the time, it was not about the car's name or type. I was proud of the fact that I set a goal and went in pursuit of making it happen. I was able to leverage the motivation it took to reach my goal. My desire to achieve my personal goal led me to become Great at my job.

Today my motivation has changed. When I was diagnosed with cancer, I prioritized what was necessary. Each day I wake up, I am motivated by objectives far more significant than a sales goal or that white Lexus. My family inspires me. I am motivated to live. On the days when I want to give up because the pain or the journey gets me down, I lean in on my purpose for living, and I press on.

As a motivated person, I fully understand that the mission is not only to achieve Greatness but also to inspire others to achieve great things. I think about this responsibility each time I step into the cancer center. When we reflect on our proudest moments and most significant achievements, they usually occur in times when motivation is at an optimal level. My most outstanding achievement was beating cancer when my life was on the line. It was easy for me to find inspiration in the middle of an extreme situation, but you don't have to wait for a severe case to motivate you to Greatness. As you strive for Greatness, if you can figure out how to push and motivate yourself, there is no limit to what can be achieved.

There is always another side to the coin, and motivation is no different. Unfortunately, some people feel that motivation is up to someone else and don't take ownership of their cause or motivational influence. Some people think there is a set standard or a universal motivational approach.

Other people have great passion and feel everyone should automatically have the same level of intensity. This is seldom the case. Either way, we must complete a self-analysis and figure out where we stand. Understanding our current position allows us to act and improve. Becoming a motivated person and becoming the Greatest version of yourself is just a decision away.

A master of motivation is also masterful at creating a climate that allows people to do their best. I had the opportunity to experience this as a high school teacher consistently. I aim to motivate and inspire as many students as possible daily. I would meet them at the door with a high five and a smile to set the tone and create positive vibrations.

Each day, a different student would start our class period with a motivational quote from the book I kept in the classroom. The goal was to have a positive interaction that motivated students to work. The key to encouraging my students was to be inspired.

Those motivated to BE THE GREATEST understand the value of motivation and can inspire a wide range of people. The Motivated knows how to push down the task and get the best out of everyone, including themselves. Motivated people empower and make each feel valued and important. They are also great leaders with whom others like to follow and enjoy working. In my case, it was my students I was seeking to motivate, but for you, it could also be family, friends, or coworkers. Creating a motivated circle will reciprocate energy that will benefit all involved.

If a motivated person wants to motivate others and create a motivated circle, they can start by simply taking an interest in the work of others and celebrating their accomplishments. A motivated person with a desire to motivate others is never too busy to acknowledge, celebrate and critique the work of others when needed. The engagement helps contribute to inspiring others and creating a motivated circle.

While we all desire to be motivated and live a motivated life, many of us fall short and are not the motivated individual we would like to be. When we fall short, it impacts the people we interact with. When you get teachers in the classroom who are not motivated, the students are the ones that are affected the most. When parents lose their motivation, the children are impacted. We all have a responsibility to check our motivation and its influence on others.

Recognizing the signs within our environment and then moving accordingly is essential. Non-motivating factors could negatively and unconsciously impact you, or you could be unmotivating others. The unmotivated don't know or care what motivates others. They usually don't bring out the best in the people around them because they are not bringing out the best within themselves. If we all lived in a shell and had no interaction with others, this would not matter, but in today's interconnected world, that is not the case. What we choose to do, impacts others.

Finding a way to harness the power of motivation is an advantage in any environment. From sports to business, motivation is a driving force for success. The lack is a recipe for disaster. Many unmotivated people believe in a one size fits all approach which contributes to not working well with people who do not like them. They are usually poor at reading others and gauging the temperature in different situations. The unmotivated also can be judgmental and stereotype others who are high performers. They also intentionally or unintentionally demotivate others leading to many not wanting to work with them. When we recognize the impact of not being motivated or being around unmotivated people, it is our responsibility to take charge and create a more motivated life.

Motivation Fundamentals:

Motivation is the engine that drives both personal and organizational success. While the need for motivation is universal, the process of motivating ourselves and others is very diverse. The key is to find what works best for you.

Create Stretch Goals. The motivated know how to leverage stretch goals. Stretch goals can be used for self-motivation and to help motivate others. Companies initially used stretch goals to motivate and inspire employees to achieve more. This usually led to a more significant return for the company.

Most people are motivated by achieving worthwhile goals. It would be best if you decided what that goal is for you. What is the plan that will push you outside of your comfort zone? Your motivation will vanish quickly if you don't lock in on a worthy goal.

Find Your Motivated Circle. Beyond self-motivation is the ability to create a motivated circle. Suppose you can find the right people for the correct position and collaborate on your stretch goals, the likelihood of motivation increases. People try their hardest when they feel they must work hard to achieve a realistic goal and they have an obligation to others. If you want to build on your motivation, find a way to incorporate or involve a team in the goal setting. You will discover another motivational layer.

Smile Often. Motivated people use the nonverbal power of a smile. A smile can go a long way to create positive vibrations in yourself and others. Find a way to keep the joy in your heart and an authentic smile. A smile disarms others and helps create a comfortable environment to reach stretch goals. People are more motivated to work harder for someone they like and respect.

If a teacher has a pleasing personality, they are more likely to inspire students. The same goals are for corporate leaders. A motivated individual can also read the body language of others to determine when additional motivational interactions are needed. A smile, wave, or thumbs up can go a long way when using nonverbals to help stimulate motivation in others and the self.

Met them where they are. To be a motivational force, you need to be able to speak the language of a variety of people on different levels. Motivation will increase when people can talk to others in a way that shows they care. All great leaders should be able to connect beyond a professional level and learn more about others. Motivated individuals can also bring others into their world to understand the perspective from a different standpoint. This perspective helps extend the trust and respect needed for further motivation.

Find your Motivational P.D.A. One of the best ways to engage motivation was revealed at the "Get Motivated Conference in Las Vegas, Nevada, when I first heard Tamara Lowe speak on motivational DNA. I love the quick, simple, easy-to-apply formula. From that day, my motivational gauge was established. She gave the audience a jewel from her book Get Motivated, which talked about Motivational DNA. I customized and leveraged the process to develop my motivational plan called P.D.A.

P- Passion – What are you passionate about? Take time to identify what you are passionate about in life. Your passion is not directly tied to any financial gain.

D- Drive & Desire – What drives you to do what you do? Take time to discover what you desire to become/accomplish or define what drives you to the next level. This will change over time as you grow as a person. Please determine what you need to live and survive, what is absolutely a necessity in your life, and how they tie to your motivation.

Accomplish & Achieve – Identify what you desire to accomplish in your life and the things you want to achieve. What do you want to accomplish, from starting a family and building a business to writing a book? What is your crown achievement? Find a significant life achievement you desire to achieve that is bigger than you. How will you implement a plan of action to achieve your considerable life accomplishments?

> Do not wait for someone else to motivate you when you can motivate yourself. You are your Greatest Motivator. Don't give that power away.

BE MOTIVATED COACHING SUPPORT QUESTIONS:

BE THE GREATEST.

WHAT STRETCH GOAL ARE YOU GOING TO ACCOMPLISH IN THE NEXT 30 TO 90 DAYS?

WHAT ARE YOU GOING TO CONSISTENTLY DO TO HELP KEEP YOURSELF MOTIVATED?

WHAT DO YOU NEED TO STOP IN EXCHANGE FOR INCREASED MOTIVATION?

WHY IS LIVING A MOTIVATED LIFESTYLE WORTH THE INVESTMENT OF RESOURCES?

The BE THE GREATEST Handbook

THOUGHTS OF GREATNESS

BE THE GREATEST.

GREATNESS DEVELOPMENT ACTION ACTIVITIES: BE THE GREATEST.

- MAP OUT YOUR NEXT STRETCH GOAL FOR THE NEXT 30 TO 90 DAYS. WRITE IT DOWN.

- CREATE YOUR MOTIVATED CIRCLE WHERE YOU CAN RECIPROCATE POSITIVE ENERGY.

- DOCUMENT YOUR MOTIVATIONAL P.D.A.
  A. WHAT ARE YOU PASSIONATE ABOUT?
  B. WHAT NEEDS DO YOU NEED TO MEET?
  C. WHAT DO YOU DESIRE TO ACHIEVE?

THOUGHTS OF GREATNESS

BE THE GREATEST.

Be Attentive

You cannot BE THE GREATEST if you are not attentive. Some might not understand the value of the development of attentiveness on the road to Greatness; however, being focused is an asset in building and maintaining relationships. No matter who you are or what you do, it is imperative to be aware of what is always happening around you. Paying attention and being attentive can be achieved by being considerate, patient, looking, and listening. When striving for Greatness, it is essential that you are open to new ideas, receptive to change, and attentive to the details.

Being attentive is the foundation of great relationships. When I evaluate my relationship with my wife and kids, the more focused I am, our relationship becomes better and stronger. By being attentive, I can show and express love to my family. I can identify changes in my children and the needs of my wife. The more I pay attention and listen to the needs and desires of my family, the more peace we have in our home. When someone feels they are not getting the time and attention they need, it is acted out somehow. Kids might exhibit attention-seeking behavior by being loud and argumentative with each other if they don't feel seen or heard. If a wife doesn't get attention from her husband, she might feel neglected and sad and seek attention elsewhere. Without awareness and quality time invested, there is no relationship.

I was eager to show off my skills and knowledge early in my professional career. I wanted people to pay attention to me and what I learned and could do. I spent little time paying attention to what was happening around me and neglected to understand how powerful being attentive was. In some ways, I tried to prove myself and used gaining attention to showcase what I could do. I was insecure and utilized my abilities to add perceived value. It never worked out in my favor, so I had to develop another strategy.

Years later, I realized I could advance further by being more attentive. I became humbler about showcasing what I knew. I got a job working for one of the biggest banks in America. I was in customer marketing and had a base salary plus a commission for exceeding the goals. The base pay was not that good, and I was driven by the incentive that was paid out monthly.

One of the first things I did when I finished training and went to my new team was to find the top performers on the team. I went and sat beside the top three for a few minutes daily. I took a jewel from each person I sat beside.

Even though I was off the phone for a period listening to others, I could apply the information and become the top salesperson in my building. Out of the 1500 people around the country who did the same job, I was ranked in the top 5 for months because I took the time to pay attention to successful clues. I even won the Quarterly Award of Excellence as a top performer and got promoted to a leadership position. Even as a top performer, I would monitor the calls of people who had certain things down better than me. I would apply the methods I knew worked versus trying to figure it out alone.

As a new high school teacher, I used attentiveness as an asset in learning how to maneuver in an academic environment. I did not take a traditional route in the classroom and had to learn many things on the job. I understood that to BE THE GREATEST teacher; I needed to be a skilled listener and take the time and the patience required to connect with my fellow teachers and students.

When I first took over as a new high school teacher, I took over a class that had already lost two teachers during the first semester. I heard horror stories about the types and other teachers' struggles. I had five different classes throughout each day. I had two classes that were upper-level students and three that were all first-year students. When I first stepped into the classroom, I was intimidated because I had heard the class run the two previous teachers off, and they quit. Substitute teachers hated that class and did not want to cover that class. Other teachers had to give up their prep period to cover this class. The teachers and the students hated it. Now it was all mine to figure out.

When I stepped into the classroom, I first noticed what was happening. It was chaos and confusion, but it wasn't because the students were terrible. The students had no direction or stable classroom leadership for two months. The morning classes were quiet and detached. The afternoon classes were wild and out of control. One class was a bit rougher than the others, 4th period. This class was right after lunch, and the students were full of energy. This was the class that was the most disliked and feared. This was the class that took pride in running off the other teachers. On the first day, I paid close attention to who the class leaders were. I wanted to know the students that had a significant influence on the class and find the best way to get them on my side.

As the class started, I always greeted students at the door. This allowed me to positively impact the students and observe their moods and attitudes daily. I was also able to give students genuine compliments and a smile that led to the foundation of our relationship. When students realized that I was paying attention to them and what was going on in their life, even my most challenging class became disarmed.

Being attentive takes patience, practice, and humility to see and hear people. I had to learn how to receive and apply information from my fellow teachers, take directives from superiors, and be available to understand student needs. As I worked to master being attentive, I learned to respect the information and opinions of others, even if I disagreed. Many people feel they must interrupt others; if they don't, it means they agree. It doesn't mean you agree. Not interrupting is respectful and shows you are being attentive and listening. Everybody wants to feel heard.

Identifying the signals of people who are not attentive is essential because they provide a great learning opportunity. People who are not attentive usually cut people off and finish others' sentences. Nonattentive people miss out on the chance to learn from others because they are not paying attention to the learning opportunities. People who don't listen and don't pay attention are often perceived as arrogant, uninterested, and impatient. In any leadership role, these perceptions can be damaging.

Some are too attentive and overuse the skill. Most of the time, we can identify these people because they spend more time listening than acting. A good listener and someone who is attentive has a balance between listening and using the information to make the appropriate decisions. Most of us know what good listening looks like.

We know not to interrupt and be able to repeat what was stated and be respectful towards others' views. The challenge for most of us is learning to listen even when we don't want to hear what is being said. It can be humbling to listen when you don't want to, but it is a necessary part of leadership.

Attentive Fundamentals: One of the pillars of being Great is the ability to be focused and to be a good listener. It is important to remember that sometimes it is best to be quiet, absorb and observe. We have two ears and a mouth. Listening twice as much as you speak should be a standard. It is impossible to simultaneously have open ears, an open mind, and an open mouth.

Listen Closely. To BE THE GREATEST version of yourself, you must maintain strong relationships. We maintain close relationships through our interactions and conversations. Often in conversation, the exchange focus on responding that we don't listen to what is being said. Or, as with others like me, we try to remember a point and don't fully listen to what the other person is speaking for fear we might forget. As we seek to deepen our relationships, we must listen to the people we desire to grow with. Once we learn to listen closely and respond, we will be one step toward mastering attentiveness.

Take notes. In today's fast-paced world, our brains are constantly overloaded with information. The more we try to remember, the more overwhelmed we become. The good thing is that we also have plenty of tools to help us remember information. Each person has a personal computer right in their pocket, allowing us to be more efficient. To help master being attentive, we can take our phones and jot down notes. It could be a phone call, a conversation, a meeting, or a date with the spouse. When you write it down, you save yourself the mental space of having to remember and free yourself to focus on other things.

Exhibit good nonverbal communication. Even when you are not using words, you can say and express a lot nonverbally. That facial expression, posture, and body language often say more than words. Make eye contact and nod to show conversation engagement. Ensure you are not looking away or checking your watch or phone consistently. After listening to what is being said, it is still wonderful to accept or reject what is displayed. The key is to do this tactfully. Remember, listening does not mean agreeing; it just means listening. Make sure you pay attention and listen.

Use and duplicate the Greatness Habit Tracker to monitor how attentive you are to your daily routine and habits. Being attentive starts with the self. Paying attention to your own life is the key to creating an attentive lifestyle.

Your Greatness is your responsibility, so Be Attentive.

The BE THE GREATEST Handbook

GREATNESS HABIT TRACKER

BE THE GREATEST.

WEEK OF: _____

	S	M	T	W	T	F	S
MORNING ROUTINE	○	○	○	○	○	○	○
EVENING ROUTINE	○	○	○	○	○	○	○
EXERCISE	○	○	○	○	○	○	○
VITAMINS	○	○	○	○	○	○	○
MEDITATION	○	○	○	○	○	○	○

NOTES

BE ATTENTIVE COACHING SUPPORT QUESTIONS:

BE THE GREATEST.

ARE YOU A GREAT LISTENER? HOW CAN YOU IMPROVE YOUR LISTENING SKILLS?

CAN YOU LISTEN WITHOUT JUDGING? WHAT CAN YOU DO TO IMPROVE?

HOW ARE YOUR NONVERBALS WHEN LISTENING? WHAT DOES YOUR BODY SAY?

WHY IS LIVING AN ATTENTIVE LIFESTYLE WORTH THE INVESTMENT OF RESOURCES?

THOUGHTS OF GREATNESS

GREATNESS DEVELOPMENT ACTION ACTIVITIES:

BE THE GREATEST.

- LISTEN TO LIVE PRESENTATIONS LIKE A SEMINAR AND TAKE DETAILED NOTES.

- LISTEN TO AUDIOBOOKS AND WRITE A BOOK REPORT SUMMING UP YOUR TAKE ALWAYS.

- HAVE A CONVERSATION WITH A FRIEND AND LET THEM TALK WHILE YOU LISTEN AND OFFER SUPPORT.

The BE THE GREATEST Handbook

THOUGHTS OF GREATNESS

BE THE GREATEST.

Ydrate Nelson, M. Ed

Be Strategic

Having an effective strategy is vital if you desire to BE THE GREATEST. The higher you want to go, or the more daunting the task, the more being strategic is essential to progression. Many people can get things done quickly, which is very important when producing short-term results, but a true visionary can string together those short-term goals for long-term success. It is like working out or adopting a new diet. You start well initially, but it will take a strategy for a real lifestyle change.

When I was diagnosed with cancer, strategic agility became more vital than ever. It was a matter of life and death. I have no choice but to become The Greatest version of myself and master being strategic. I was forced to map out the direction of the future I wanted to see. I had to predict the trends and use my vast knowledge and perspectives to make the right decisions. I had to create life-altering strategies to keep my life progressively moving forward. If my plan didn't work, my life would be threatened.

When I decided to forgo traditional cancer treatments for more non-traditional approaches in my cancer battle, I had to come up with a strategy that I felt comfortable with and assured my loved ones I had a real plan to save my life. I knew some things were beyond my control, so I focused on strategizing on the things I could. When I first got my diagnosis, I was also prediabetic and overweight. I know that my ability to beat cancer was based on my ability to build my body up, get healthy and lose weight. Over the few years before my diagnosis, I formed terrible health habits. I was not working out regularly and eating what I wanted when I wanted to. Realizing I needed to change was obvious but how to go about it was a struggle. I could not just change and get better overnight. I needed a plan that was sustainable for the long run.

I knew I had to adjust but was overwhelmed with information and directives. I was trying to do many things at the same time. I was changing my diet, working out daily, and adopting a vegan diet with no sugar while being a husband, father, employee, and entrepreneur. I lived in a constant state of exhaustion. I was doing way too much each day. When I reached a point of extreme overwhelm, I would end up dropping the ball on everything I was doing.

After trying various things that didn't stick to the wall and operating without a strategy, I became more vulnerable. It was not until I sat down and started to map out a real plan to beat cancer. I started by controlling my diet. I decided to activate intermittent fasting back into my lifestyle first. I would have an 8-hour window and fast for 16 hours daily. To help keep me focused, I downloaded an app that tracked how long I fasted daily. It gave me updates for each hour I fasted so I could see what my body was doing as I fasted. Using this app was an aid that helped me take control of my eating and diet.

The next step in the operation to beat cancer was increasing my exercise by walking 10,000 steps daily. I purchased a watch I could wear most of the time to track my steps, sleep, and heart rate. Having the watch on gave me a quick way to keep track of my efforts. As soon as I hit my goal, the watch would buzz to let me know the daily goal was reached. I was less conscious of my steps and overall health when I didn't have my watch. The watch became part of my strategy to get my steps in to improve my health.

My body was deficient in various areas when I first got my bloodwork after being diagnosed. I was not very big on taking pills and had taken very few over my life. I was put in a position where I had to find ways to get my body back to optimal health and boost my immune system. The first thing I did was to look and see what was abnormally high and low in my blood. After I saw what was out of range, I would look up the natural remedies that would allow me to improve my deficiencies. I started to eat different foods and take a ton of supplements. After each blood panel, I would modify and plan to combat the negative impacts. I learned to listen to my body and map out the plan to improve my health.

I made a list of everything I put into my body and monitored the impact. I would adjust if something did not agree with my body or made me feel a certain way. I ended up taking about 20 supplement pills per day. I even had to create a strategy of what to take and when to take it. Some therapeutics require food, and some do not. I must work on certain pills around my fasting time and devise a plan to help me secure my health. If I didn't take the time to strategize and come up with a real plan, I would have gotten overwhelmed and given up. That could have been deadly. Being strategic was not just a matter of execution to get things done but a life-or-death mission.

Before my diagnosis, I didn't think or act with a specific health strategy. I was not thinking about mapping out long-term plans that are progressive. My lack of exposure or experience in fighting cancer and living healthy was the culprit for the lack of strategic thinking. My focus was on business, and I neglected to be strategically agile regarding health. That lack of focused thought needed for growth could have cost me my life.

Action Based Fundamentals

Embrace strategic planning. Many people reject strategic planning because it has never worked for them or they have never seen a long-term strategy executed. The fact that most plans don't work out exactly how they are drafted can be discouraging to some. The truth is that all good plans require modifications, and adjustments are part of the process. Without a strategy, there would be no clear path to the results. People and organizations who don't embrace strategic planning will soon find themselves in the dark.

Buy strategic time by delegating. Most people are often inundated with busy tasks and time restrictions. The more they try to do, the less that gets done. Most of the time, strategic planning falls to the bottom of the list if it makes a list. When people are great delegators, they can multiply their efforts by having others help them get things done. The more help and assistance a manager have with the daily task, the more time they must focus on strategic planning. No company has ever reached a significant milestone by accident. Delegate to create the time needed for effective strategic planning.

Be imaginative; think futuristic. Being THE GREATEST requires imagination and a forward-thinking mentality. In most scenarios, there is a need for results today. The urgency puts more emphasis on the moment over the plans. Many people use their imagination to think about problems that might arise *instead of* a strategy for the future because without results today, there might not be a future. To help develop a broader perspective beyond the typical thoughts, study great innovators, join leadership organizations and consult with others about their ideas for the future. For most people, the answers they need are right under their noses in the form of those they manage. Don't be afraid to ask those you work with for ideas about progression and the future.

GREATNESS GOAL PLANNER — BE THE GREATEST.

MY GREATNESS GOAL:

MY WHY:

START DATE:

ACHIEVE BY:

ACTION STEPS TO GREATNESS:

- ....
- ....
- ....
- ....
- ....
- ....

NOTES & GREAT IDEAS:

Ydrate Nelson, M. Ed

BE STRATEGIC COACHING SUPPORT QUESTIONS:

BE THE GREATEST.

WHAT CAN YOU PERSONALLY DO TO HELP EMBRACE MORE STRATEGIC PLANNING?

WHAT TASKS CAN YOU DELEGATE TO TO CREATE TIME FOR STRATEGIC PLANNING?

WHO CAN YOU PARTNER WITH TO SHARE IDEAS FOR A MORE STRATEGIC PERSPECTIVE?

WHAT TYPE OF SCALE WILL YOU USE TO TRACK YOUR STRATEGIC VIABILITY?

THOUGHTS OF GREATNESS

BE THE GREATEST.

GREATNESS DEVELOPMENT ACTION ACTIVITIES: BE THE GREATEST.

PARTNER WITH OTHERS STRIVING FOR GREATNESS AND CREATE A JOINT VENTURE.

CHART THE IDEAS THAT YOU FEEL WILL HELP MOVE LIFE FORWARD AND PRESENT THEM TO YOUR GREATNESS CIRCLE.

RESEARCH PREVIOUS COMPANIES, CASE STUDIES, OR SIMILAR SITUATIONS THAT ARE PARALLEL TO PRESENT OR FORECASTED PROBLEMS ISSUES TO USE AS GUIDE.

THOUGHTS OF GREATNESS

BE THE GREATEST.

Be a Master Communicator

To reach the heights of Greatness, you must be a great communicator. A leader with a problem articulating directions presents challenges for those who follow. While different people have different communication strengths, there still must be a balance between spoken, written, and nonverbal communication to BE THE GREATEST. I have been able to elevate my life in various ways based on my ability to Be a Master Communicator. Every job advancement and leadership opportunity has been based on my ability to be a master communicator.

My first professional job was for a company called MCI which sold long-distance phone service over the phone. This was before the days when each person had a personal computer in their pocket. This is where I learned the power of communication using my words only. The people on the other end of the phone never saw my face. They only heard my voice. I realized the power of language and the power of a smile over the phone. I learned that how you say something is just as important as what you say. I also learned to recognize other people's tones as I attempted to connect and close sales.

It was not until about a decade later, when I was hired to work for a central bank, that I was able to capitalize on the power of verbal communication. We were trained and encouraged to use powerful words in our conversations over the phone. I was introduced to the power of delightful words. I would use simple words in conversation like wonderful, magnificent, amazing, outstanding, and beautiful. I still use all the words in my daily conversation to this day. This is where I learned the power of a smile even when you are not visible. The people on the other line could hear my smile and joy. I could leverage powerful words and effective communication to become a top performer.

After being a top performer for about a year, I had the opportunity to get promoted. Once again, I leveraged the power of communication to elevate. As soon as I walked into the room for the interview with 3 of the managers I would be working with, I had a big smile. Even in the formalities and introduction, I used delightful words in my conversation. After the first interview, the decision was made; I got the promotion that put me in a position over the 600 people who were once my peers.

This was when I joined Toastmasters, which emphasized developing public speaking and leadership skills. I felt I was good as a communicator, but I wanted to improve. I won over ten different speaking contests. I was also able to advance from a new member to the club president to the area governor with the personal and professional development of employees from companies that included the University of Phoenix, American Express, Capital One, and others.

I had over 125 people who followed my leadership to become better speakers and leaders. Being an effective communicator helped me build the trust and respect that made others comfortable with my leadership. There is a direct connection between being an effective communicator and leadership.

When I transitioned into the classroom from corporate America, my ability to effectively communicate with my students helped me develop relationships that positively impacted the students' experience. Before I ever said a word to any student, I would greet them at the door with a smile and a high five. When they saw my smile followed by a high five, they all felt positive energy and communicated that my classroom was a positive learning environment. I could leverage my positive communication skills to get the most out of my students. I could master communication which took me from being a part-time substitute to the Teacher of the year.

I learned that people skilled at communication could clearly articulate a message using various methods. They can get the news across that has the intended effect. People who are master communicators understand the value of being able to use a variety of communication methods to deliver a message. This is why I would spend extra time greeting, high-fiving, and listening to my students. I knew that even though I was not speaking a word initially, I was communicating a powerful message.

On the flip side, I have also witnessed and know some people who lack communication. People who are unskilled at communication often struggle in leadership roles and relationships because they have difficulty reaching objectives. Often, those who don't work on becoming better communicators have difficulty articulating the point, may be too wordy, too short in explanation, or may not have a logical argument. Too often strive for perfection when the key is to communicate honest, heartfelt answers.

Action-Based Communication Fundamentals

Focus on creating an outline. A Master of Communication should never speak or send a written communication without having some direction or articulated aim of the message. That is why having an outline is vital. An outline allows you to create a checklist to ensure that all points are effectively communicated. This ensures that each delivered moment is memorable and not fluff. Sticking to the outline helps keep the plan on track and increases the likelihood of success.

Know your target audience. When delivering any message, it is vital to know who the audience is or whom you are speaking to. A great communicator understands that communication is not one size fits all. The differences between the audiences receiving a message must be identified. The same message can be delivered to different classes if the uniqueness of each group can be isolated. The speed of delivery, tone, and length must be adjusted to communicate the message to the audience effectively.

Use powerful language. What you say is just as important as how you say it. Whether writing or speaking, words need to be robust and rememberable. Use words that add meaning and power to the presentation. Avoid space-consuming jargon that adds no value to the point. When working on using powerful language, it is imperative to use your voice. While creativity can be an asset, using words and language that is not authentic can hurt the message more than help it.

Effective communication is not only the link between ignorance and enlightenment but also the key to success in life, business, and personal relationships. The more effective the communication, the higher the chances for Greatness.

BE A M.C. COACHING SUPPORT QUESTIONS:

BE THE GREATEST.

WHAT CAN YOU DO TO IMPROVE VERBAL COMMUNICATION SKILLS?

WHAT CAN YOU DO TO IMPROVE NONVERBAL COMMUNICATION SKILLS?

HOW CAN YOU CONSISTENTLY DEVELOP ON ALL LEVELS OF COMMUNICATION?

WHAT CAN YOU DO TO ENSURE THAT YOU HOLD THE ATTENTION OF YOUR AUDIENCE TO DEILVER YOUR MESSAGE?

THOUGHTS OF GREATNESS

BE THE GREATEST.

GREATNESS DEVELOPMENT ACTION ACTIVITIES:

BE THE GREATEST.

FOCUS ON YOUR PERSONAL CONVERSATIONS, EVALUATE, AND SEEK TO FIND A WAY TO IMPROVE COMMUNICATION SKILLS.

WRITE A BUSINESS EMAIL OR A LETTER TO A LOVED ONE AND HAVE SOMEONE READ IT AND GIVE FEEDBACK.

WORK ON VERBAL AND NON-VERBAL COMMUNICATION BY RECORDING YOURSELF SPEAKING AND PAY ATTENTION TO WHAT YOUR VERBALS ARE SAYING.

THOUGHTS OF GREATNESS

BE THE GREATEST.

Be Trustworthy

Trust is in the profile of every person of Greatness, so it is fair to say you can't be Great if you can't be trusted. Trust is the foundation for all great relationships and teams. Without trust, many relationships would not have value or matter to those involved. You can't BE THE GREATEST if people don't buy into what you say because of a lack of integrity and trust. A lack of confidence makes it difficult to accomplish goals because people don't want to serve or assist those they can't trust.

When I look at all the roles I have been privileged to be in; trust has been vital to my success. I have worked in leadership roles in corporate America, in sales positions, and even as a teacher in the classroom. Each role requires trustworthiness for success. Over the last decade, I won several mentoring/community awards for working with the youth and serving my community. These awards included the Bank of America Local Hero Award, The Mitch Akin Mentor of the year award, the P.A.L.S. Mentor of the Year, the 2019 Difference Maker Award, and most recently, the 2020 Teacher of the Year. Each role allowed me to succeed and show up as the Greatest version of myself because the community and people I served trusted me. Without respect, there is no trust, and without faith, there is no success.

As an inexperienced classroom teacher, I learned the value of trust and honesty early. In my first year in the classroom, I was teaching a subject I had no experience or education in, science. There were many questions that students asked that I didn't know the answer to. If it were an opinioned based question, I would do my best to answer it to the best of my ability. If there were a science-related question that I didn't know, I would respond with, "that's a great question that I don't have the answer to, but I will follow up and have a solution for you shortly. Students respected that I would be honest and follow up with the correct answer.

I would research the question or go to another teacher I trusted to assist. Once I got the answer, I would then relay the answer back to the class. This helped establish the trust I needed to facilitate a thriving learning environment.

It is vital for anyone striving to BE THE GREATEST to embrace being trustworthy and build trust within their students, teams, organizations, relationships, or anyone they encounter. Responsible people are respected, seen as direct, can admit mistakes, and take responsibility. They keep their confidence and do not misrepresent themselves for personal or short-term gains at the expense of others.

Those individuals who are not trustworthy hurt everyone they encounter. They can easily be identified because they make promises they don't or can't keep and blame others for their mistakes. They lack follow-through and may treat others differently. Many people perceive this type of person as selfish and not worthy of trust and respect. This hurts cohesiveness and diminishes the trust needed for optimal results. In any environment, there is no success if there is no trust. Many people who struggle in leadership roles usually don't have the trust of the people they are working with.

Build Trust: Building trust is a process that takes time and patience. The foundation for establishing trust is doing what needs to be done and saying what needs to be told, no matter how difficult it might be. Speaking with confidence and making good eye contact helps build and maintain trust. Don't hesitate and know what you will say before speaking. Don't ever exaggerate or overpromise anything you can't guarantee.

Being enthusiastic is one thing, but making a promise you can't keep is lying. That is a quick way to destroy trust. Don't be afraid to be honest if you can't honor a request. If you miscalculate times or promises, go back, and inform the parties involved as soon as it is realized. Avoid putting yourself in impossible situations. It is better to under-promise and over-deliver than to overpromise and under-deliver. One with help build your trust, and the other will help destroy it.

A trustworthy person is a master at keeping the confidence of others. Trusted people often get a great deal of personal information disclosed to them. Even one slip-up can lead to mistrust that may never be restored. Ask for clarity if there is a question about what can or can't be shared. Don't be afraid to accept responsibility if there is a conflict or misunderstanding. Never blame others or blindside anyone. Maintain integrity and do what you feel is right. At times this might be difficult.

Many of my students would share various things with me as a teacher. I worked hard to establish trust so I could be an ally to as many students as possible. One day a student disclosed something I was obligated to report. She told me in confidence after a promise not to share the information. After she told me, I was confused about what to do, so I called one of the teacher mentors I trusted and asked me what to do. He told me that I needed to report what I knew immediately.

At this point, I was stuck between breaking the student's trust and getting further assistance to help the student. I knew the student had trust issues and didn't want to complicate that further. I had to be delicate with how I dealt with this situation because there was a trust issue with the student and liability as an educator.

When I returned to school, I went to an administrator to ask about the best way to move forward with the information. I informed them that the students have trust issues with adults, and I didn't want to harm her comfort by sharing information in the future. I asked them to allow me to speak with her first before they pulled her aside and took action. I informed the student that the information she shared with me required that I get other people involved and, if I didn't, it could be a liability. The student told me that she had never told anyone; even her parents didn't know because it would negatively impact her family if they found out.

I explained that I could be present when she spoke with the counselor or social workers and aid her in any way, but I could not just let her suffer without attempting to get her some help to deal with her situation. The student was embarrassed and initially not comfortable. I explained that I was honored that she trusted me, but I would be hurting her if I didn't help her. The student was very emotional but was glad she could get the issue she had been holding for years off her chest.

Due to the nature of the situation, I never discussed it with the student. She came to class, and at first, she was more distant in style and became very quiet. After a while, she came to me and said she was getting help and was glad I acted. She told her parents, and they got involved in getting her the help she needed.

At first, I was concerned I was breaking a student's trust and felt inadequate or like I was making a mistake by betraying her trust. In this case, it worked out, and I could maintain the established faith, but that's not always the case. Mistakes are bound to happen, but the best way to ensure confidence is not broken or restored is to communicate with all parties involved expeditiously.

Publicly acknowledge mistakes and take personal responsibility when required. Make sure you don't dwell on the mistakes and move on from them. People who admit their mistakes are often perceived as more trustworthy and competent. Admitting errors also shows humility which is an excellent complement to being trustworthy.

Sometimes it's hard to trust other people's words,

Sometimes it's even hard to trust others' actions,

But always trust your instincts.

Building Trust Fundamentals:

Effective Communication: When working on building trust as a person, several core elements can be incorporated. Make sure that as you work to develop and establish trust, you are communicating things that need to be relayed. Make an effort to ensure that every person involved is well informed on what needs to know—master timing to ensure that complex messages are delivered considerately. Make sure you follow up and return calls and emails.

Restore Trust: Restoring trust can be a very humbling experience. The best way to restore trust is to admit your mistake or misstep and ask for forgiveness. Find out if there is a way for redemption or to rebuild the trust that has been lost. Make sure you can speak to what went wrong and a solution for the future. Also, find out what needs to be stopped and if the relationship can be repaired.

Be Selfless and Respectful: When building trust as a leader, ensure you put the team first and your ego and emotions to the side. Share the credit with those involved. Be a mentor and a coach to those looking to grow and prosper. When teams trust leadership, the effort increases, leading to better results. People are also more likely to trust people that respect them and whom they have respect for. If there is no respect, there is no trust.

You were created to be Great. Always trust and believe in yourself. You have survived everything you have ever been through and will continue to do so. Don't let the troubles of this world get you down. Keep confidence in yourself, faith in your higher power, trust in the process and BE THE GREATEST.

BE TRUSTWORTHY SUPPORT QUESTIONS:

BE THE GREATEST.

WHAT MAKES YOU TRUSTWORTHY?

WHAT CAN YOU DO TO BUILD MORE TRUST IN YOUR RELATIONSHIPS?

HOW CAN YOU BUILD TRUST AND AUTHORITY WHEN YOU SPEAK?

HOW DO YOU RESTORE TRUST WHEN IT IS BROKEN? HOW DO YOU SHARE YOUR STRATEGY WITH OTHERS?

The BE THE GREATEST *Handbook*

THOUGHTS OF GREATNESS

BE THE GREATEST.

GREATNESS DEVELOPMENT ACTION ACTIVITIES: BE THE GREATEST.

SPEAK WITH AUTHORITY AND CONFIDENCE IN YOUR CONVERSATIONS. MAKE EYE CONTACT AND SMILE WHEN FACE TO FACE.

FIND SOMEONE YOU HAVE DISAPPOINTED OR HAD A CONFLICT WITH AND MAKE PEACE AND PRACTICE RESTORING TRUST.

BE CAREFUL WITH PROMISES. BE TRUE TO YOUR WORD AND FOLLOW THROUGH WITH YOUR ACTIONS. THE POINT OF BUILDING TRUST IS FOR OTHERS TO BELIEVE WHAT YOU SAY SO HONOR YOUR WORD.

THOUGHTS OF GREATNESS

BE THE GREATEST.

Be Savvy

Being interpersonal savvy is a must in your quest to BE THE GREATEST. As you learn to Stand in your Greatness, you will develop the capacity to deal with and work with various people. Being savvy requires being able to neutralize personal feelings to ensure others are being heard and respected. Mastering interpersonal savvy will allow you to overcome objections that enable you to get what you need without doing harm that would cause the other party not to desire to work with you.

People skilled at being savvy usually relate well to all kinds of people within an organization and outside the community. They can build the appropriate rapport needed to help establish trust. Masters of savvy are tactful, diplomatic, and able to make constructive and effective relationships. When you become the Greatest version of yourself, you are also masterful at using interpersonal savvy to defuse high-stress and tension-related situations that can be uncomfortable.

I have always worked well with various people, but working in telecommunications and sales helped elevate my interpersonally savvy. I had to work with multiple people and figure out how to meet each person where they were. When working for one of the largest banks in America, I worked in a department known as customer marketing. Customers would call in to get their credit cards activated.

When they called in, my job was to activate their cards and upscale them on one of the bank's products. Customers didn't call in to be sold a product, just to activate their credit card. I had to learn how to integrate a sale into the conversation. The customers were very diverse. They ranged from people with little financial resources to those with plenty.

Some days I would talk to hundreds of people from around the country. I learned how to pick up on their tone and adjust my conversation to meet them where they were at that moment. People from the northeast United States talked at a different pace than people from the south and other areas of the country.

I would always start out using powerful delight words to open the interaction. My goal was to get the sale, but each call was diverse and unique. I leveled up my game because it directly impacted my income. I never wanted to be pushy, rude, or make the customer feel uncomfortable, but, at the same time, I wanted to make sales because I was compensated extra for every deal closed.

By learning to be interpersonal savvy, I was able to almost triple my salary during my first year on the job. At my highest, I was ranked 3 out of over 1500 people. A year later, I was promoted because of my ability to connect with various people. I had the privilege to work with three different departments and over 600 people each week because of my ability to understand the process of multiple divisions while training people on different skill levels. My interpersonal savvy development was vital in elevating my position.

When I first became a teacher, I quickly realized the importance of being savvy in high school. In my first year, I had over 150 students ranging from the 9th to the 12th grade. Students were from multiple races, cultures, and economic backgrounds. There would be days when one student would come up and celebrate a significant accomplishment, while the next would be heartbroken from a breakup or personal tragedy.

The goal was to find a way to make each student feel heard and seen no matter what their situation was. I would often have to juggle and manage the emotional state of a variety of students while still maintaining my composure. Students felt respected and valued. Even though I was a new teacher, I still achieved the teacher of the semester because of my ability to connect with and elevate students by applying my mastery of interpersonal savvy.

Non-Savvy people have a hard to relating well to a variety of people. They often have a hard time building meaningful relationships. Unsavvy people may be a bit raw and too direct at times. They may appear impatient and arrogant and may not read others well. Non-savvy people may panic or freeze when faced with adversity or conflict. Whether you are a high school teacher, work in a corporate office, or any leadership role, become a master of interpersonal savvy.

Lacking interpersonal savvy skills in today's world is a liability. It is vital to find a way to communicate, understand, and collaborate while allowing space for objective thought and opposing points of view. Mastering interpersonal savvy is the key to building community and maintaining diverse relationships.

Savvy Fundamentals:

Be Flexible but unbreakable. The first step to mastering interpersonal savvy is to be flexible and embrace change. Even though we are all created equal, we are all still individuals, very different and unique. Flexibility allows you to connect with various people and get the task done without being locked into a fixed mindset. Sometimes it is necessary to tailor an approach to fit the needs of others as long as it does not compromise your values. That is why it is essential to pay attention to the needs of others and make sure that you understand when to be flexible and when to stay firm so you don't compromise yourself.

Set the tone. A savvy person understands the importance of setting the tone. When individuals set the tone, they have more control over the first impression. A good first impression makes a person more approachable and puts others at ease when disclosing information. Being a great listener is essential to mastering interpersonal savvy because listening helps the leader understand before responding. A skilled leader also makes sure that nonverbal matches the verbal. Nodding and eye contact is excellent ways to use nonverbal communication while mastering interpersonal savvy.

Embrace Diversity. A master of savvy is comfortable in a variety of settings and embraces diversity. When you are stuck in your comfort zone, you are not forced to grow and can maneuver inside a small window. When you step outside of that comfort zone, you must expand your ability to connect with people in different environments—simple things like going to a new restaurant in another culture and communicating with the people inside. Take a trip to a new country or city in a different part of the country or world and indulge in the culture. Embracing a new culture and diversity will not only help you become savvier but also help you BE THE GREATEST version of yourself.

When you have outstanding interpersonal savvy, people will follow your path no matter the distance and follow your leadership no matter the height of the standard.

BE SAVVY COACHING SUPPORT QUESTIONS:

BE THE GREATEST.

WHAT MAKES YOU A SAVVY PERSON?

HOW DO YOU WORK WITH PEOPLE YOU DON'T LIKE? HOW CAN YOU IMPROVE?

DO YOU THINK PEOPLE GENUINELY ENJOY WORKING WITH AND BEING AROUND YOU? WHY?

HOW DO YOU DEVELOP YOUR INTERPERSONAL SKILLS ON A PERSONAL AND PROFESSIONAL LEVEL?

THOUGHTS OF GREATNESS

BE THE GREATEST.

GREATNESS DEVELOPMENT ACTION ACTIVITIES: BE THE GREATEST.

WORK WITH SOMEONE YOU DON'T HAVE ANYTHING IN COMMON WITH OR DON'T LIKE TO GET A PROJECT DONE.

TAKE RESPONSIBILITY FOR DELIVERING A HARD MESSAGE OR SOME DISTURBING NEWS IN A COMPASSIONATE AND SAVVY WAY.

GO TO A NEW RESTAURANT FROM ANOTHER CULTURE AND COMMUNICATE WITH THE PEOPLE INSIDE. TAKE A TRIP TO A NEW COUNTRY AND EMBRACE THE LOCAL COMMUNITY CULTURE.

THOUGHTS OF GREATNESS

BE THE GREATEST.

Ydrate Nelson, M. Ed

Be Compassionate

The world, workplace, and corporate America can be cold, and we need compassionate individuals. Unfortunately, being a good person is a foreign concept for many people. Many people feel that compassion and work don't mix. Life will happen to us all at some point, and compassion is a tool that we all need in the tool kit. We never know what someone else is going through, so we must lead with compassion.

While working as a high school teacher in my first year, I taught three class periods of freshmen science. In my first-year freshman class, I would have a few seniors who failed their freshmen year and now need to make up classes to graduate. I was never hard on the upper-level students. I treated them less strictly because they had already been at the school for four years. I just made sure they had graduated and turned in their work. I was not going to allow them to fail twice, and I also understood the seniors would be 17 or 18 in the class with students 14 and 15-year-olds students.

In my 6th-period freshmen science class, I had one senior.

He was reticent and often slept in class. I didn't bother him much if he turned in his work. One day, the teacher across the walkway, who also had the same student, asked me about the student's classroom activity. The teacher said, "man, this student sleeps in my class every day and is not turning in all his work. If he doesn't pick it up, he won't pass my class or graduate." He then asked me about my relationship with the student. I told him I felt as if we had a great relationship. He asked if I would speak with him about his classroom activity and encourage him to stay awake and be more active in class.

That very same day, I got stricter with the student and told him that he needed to be more active in all his classes. I didn't tell him about the conversation with the other teacher; I just gave him some advice that applied to all his classes. He looked at me and said I would pick it up and do better. Each time he went to sleep, I would come by and wake him up and put him back on task. About a week later, I went over to the teacher I had the original conversation with and informed him that I spoke with the student—the student committed to picking up his activity in all classes.

The teacher looked at me and then dropped his head. He lifted his head, looked me in the face, and said, "I feel like a complete ass. I was riding this student about sleeping in class, and I discovered that he and his younger sister were living out of their car. He stays up at night so his sister can sleep. He feels safe and comfortable when he comes to school and gets the rest he can't get at night."

At that moment, I felt like an ass as well. I had no idea what was happening with the student and was quick to judge the student when I didn't know the whole story. I then reflected on how many other students might be dealing with similar situations, and I had no clue. From that day, moving forward, I started to grant my students more grace and compassion. When I would see a student sleeping in class a lot, I would no longer assume they were being disrespectful or lazy. I would pull them aside to check to see if they were ok. That one student changed the way I conducted myself in the classroom.

I created a classroom culture that made students feel safe and comfortable with each other to the point that they would check on each other before I did. Being a more compassionate teacher helped create and classroom culture of compassion that my students adopted.

Compassionate people genuinely care about others and are concerned about their work and non-work-related issues. They are usually available and willing to help when necessary. Skilled and compassionate people know the right time to demonstrate empathy and understanding. They also know how to empathize with the less fortunate and show humility.

One area of life that is near and dear to me is working with the homeless. I do my best to invest time and effort as I support a small part in helping our most vulnerable citizens. While working as a high school teacher a few years ago, I drove for a rideshare company over the summer while school was out for teachers. I woke up early to start my day and got my first call around 8:15 am. A lady needed a ride from the west side of Phoenix to downtown. I went and picked her up and took her to her destination, a courthouse near the capital. This morning, even though it was early, it was still boiling. I had my AC on for my rider and me.

After dropping her off, I passed right by the homeless camp downtown. I was passing by with my air conditioner on full blast, and it was barely 9 am. I thought about how hard it was to be homeless and not have the luxury of escaping into an air-conditioned room. I drove around and picked up passengers for half instead of working the whole day. I then took the money I made that day and bought as many cases of water as possible. I then went to the homeless district and passed out as many bottles as possible. On the first day did over 200 bottles.

I told one of my co-workers, who was also a high school teacher, about my mission, and a few days later, he joined me along with his son as we went back to the district to pass out more bottles. I repeated this process a few times and continued to show compassion to our vulnerable citizens. As people learn about my mission to hydrate the homeless, they will contribute to water and hygiene products. By the end of the summer, I had personally given out over 2,000 bottles of water directly from my car.

A few months later, I was out hanging out with my younger brother Donald Jr. and one of my closest friends Quentin Henry who was visiting me in Phoenix, AZ. We decided before we spent time hanging out that we would do some community service. We got some bottled water and pizza and went to the streets.

We came across a gentle who was touched by our decision to come out and show them love and support. He found out I was a high school teacher and asked if I could record a video message he had for the students. Even though he was living on the streets, he showed compassion to my students so they would not end up in his situation.

I took the video back and showed it to my students. Many of them were touched, and some of them decided to act. The students decided to put together some care packages for them. We collected toiletry items, water, and things students thought might be helpful to those on the streets. We could put together almost 200 care packages and give them directly to the people on the streets. This all evolved my me showing compassion.

Non-compassionate people appear to be less caring and empathetic than most. They don't take the time to probe and ask personal questions. They believe in the separation between personal and business life. Others feel they don't want to get consumed by non-work-related issues. People who don't develop compassion believe that results are all that matter and don't factor in the human element. People with little heart can be poison to a team and work environment.

> Don't overexert yourself showing other people compassion and neglect yourself. If you truly want to live a compassionate life, start with yourself, and make it a lifestyle and not just an act or gesture. Let compassion be who you are and not just what you do.

Compassion Fundamentals

Develop a Daily Self Compassion routine. Before showing compassion to others, you much first be compassionate to yourself. Many people find it easier to show compassion to others than to themselves. If you want to show up and BE THE GREATEST version of yourself, you must find ways to BE Compassionate and not just show compassion to others. If we develop a human relationship with ourselves, it becomes a lifestyle that happens without effort. Increase your prayer and meditation time. Incorporate nature walks and spend some time journaling to catalog your thoughts. Take yourself on a date and do more things you love. Before you consider helping others, take time to help and love yourself first.

Show more Empathy. The first step to improving compassion is to start by showing more empathy. Listen to what others have to say. Many times, people need to talk it out. Keep eye contact and nod to show you are listening. Respond when appropriate with helpful value-added feedback. Delay too much advice giving unless you are asked. Listening can be a more valuable gesture than speaking.

As you listen, put yourself in their shoes. How would you feel? What would you do? What can you do to help? Offer practical help if possible. Most of the time, people need a listening ear, an open mind, and a heart, if nothing else provide hope for a better day because sometimes that's the most valuable thing we can offer.

Set your limits. Make sure your set limits. You are not a counselor and don't want to get tied up with everybody's problems. That can be frustrating and draining. Be brief and show compassion at the same time. When they start to repeat, summarize to indicate you heard and are listening. Suggest additional resources if a problem is more significant than your capability. If you are short on time, invite us to speak later to finish the conversation or offer other options if applicable.

Compassion is an unspoken connection that transcends religions, spoken languages, races, ethnicity, and education. Compassion is a boundless wave of continuous energy that sends the positive vibrations needed to build the foundation of humanity.

BE COMPASSIONATE SUPPORT QUESTIONS:

BE THE GREATEST.

HOW DO YOU BUILD YOURSELF TO BE A MORE COMPASSIONATE PERSON?

HOW GOOD ARE YOU AT LISTENING WITHOUT GIVING ADVICE? WHAT WOULD HAPPEN IF YOU IMPROVED IN THIS AREA?

HOW DO YOU HANDLE TENSE SITUATIONS? WHAT COULD YOU DO TO IMPROVE HOW YOU HANDLE STRESSFUL SITUATIONS AND THE PEOPLE INVOLVED?

HOW COULD YOU BE MORE EMPATHETIC WHEN DEALING WITH OTHER PEOPLE'S NEEDS AND PROBLEMS?

THOUGHTS OF GREATNESS

GREATNESS DEVELOPMENT ACTION ACTIVITIES: BE THE GREATEST.

- JOIN A SELF-HELP GROUP AS A SPONSOR OR SUPPORT FOR SOMEONE ELSE.

- VOLUNTEER AT A LOCAL CHARITY HELPING THE LESS FORTUNATE.

- WORK ON A PROJECT THAT MUST MAKE TOUGH DECISIONS ABOUT THE FUTURE OF OTHERS. PUT ASIDE PERSONAL FEELINGS AND ONLY CONSIDER WHAT IS BETTER THE GROUP BEING SERVED.

THOUGHTS OF GREATNESS

BE THE GREATEST.

Ydrate Nelson, M. Ed

Be Creative

To BE THE GREATEST, you must also be creative. Creativity is a very underrated skill that most people don't feel they have. Many people usually associate creativity with the arts, like music or painting. However, organizations need creative people to help problem solve and introduce new ideas. Creativity is also required to stay innovative and maintain a competitive edge. New products and services exist because of creative minds. Many people have been taught to be focused, refined and narrow in scope. Over time this can take away from the flexibility needed to remain creative. When creativity is at an all-time high, people are likelier to stay engaged and productive.

While working in education, I often leveraged my creative mind to create classroom culture. I needed a way to keep my students engaged in class. I realized that many students started the week off slow and with low energy, and on Fridays, many seniors didn't come to class. I was losing two days of productivity per week from disengagement and absences. This was making a difficult job even more difficult. I had to find a way to keep students engaged in getting the most out of them.

I created themed days to increase classroom enthusiasm. Each Monday was the theme Mindset Motivation Monday. We would review the previous week each Monday, laying out what the coming week would look like. I would spend a considerable chunk of class empowering and encouraging my students to be focused throughout the entire week.

Each Tuesday was Term Up Tuesday. On this day, we would review words from the previous week and add new vocabulary words for the lesson we would cover over the coming week. Each Wednesday was Wonderful Wednesday, a collaboration day. Students would work in groups or with a partner to complete a project or review and student for the up-and-coming test.

Thursday was known as Triumphant Thursday and on the only day of the week when we would have exams, tests, or major projects due. Each Friday was Freestyle Friday. On this day, I would freestyle and rap for the students if we were done with all activities for the week. I never started a new lesson on Friday, so we would finish the task for the week and use the remainder of the time to do some fun class activities. At one point, Friday was the week's day with the most absent student. After the introduction of freestyle Friday, attendance for that day went up. As a result of being creative in the classroom, I could make the class more enjoyable and productive. Outside the school, I kept my themed days as part of my lifestyle and shared them with others.

Someone skilled in creativity usually comes up with new ideas and ways of doing things. They can problem solve by finding new solutions to old problems. This quality is valuable in any personal or work environment. Creatively skilled individuals add value to any group they are in because of their original perspective and ability to think outside of the box.

Unskilled people in creativity are usually on the conservative side and often overly cautious. They are often more comfortable with the past and not comfortable fostering new ideas. When people lack creativity, they avoid taking chances and risks. They seek to blend in and shy away from being bold and unique. A lack of creativity also leads to strained team dynamics because an open mind is needed to work with various people. Some people generally have no idea how creativity works and may unintentionally kill the creativity of others. When we don't embrace creativity, we welcome problems.

Creativity Fundamentals

Being able to tap into creative thought is a valuable leadership quality. Even those who are considered skilled at being creative can always get better. Most of the time, creativity is right beneath the surface. You just need to unleash the restraints. Creative thinking does not follow traditional thought patterns or the rules of logic. For many leaders, this can be a scary thought.

Brainstorm The easiest way to get the creative juices flowing is to start brainstorming. Find a problem, issue, concern, or goal you desire to accomplish. Start by writing everything down that you can about the chosen item. For example, if you wanted to start a new business, you might start by thinking of different names and logos. No idea is a bad idea. Just write and record everything. Then, narrow down the list and refine it until you are left with the best of the best. From there, you can further your creativity by getting input from others to see what value they can add to their creativity. Brainstorming is not designed to be a clean and neat process, so don't worry about editing and refining initially. Write down as much information as possible.

Solve a Problem. Next, find a problem that needs a solution. It could be a project around the house or a challenge at work. Instead of looking at what cannot be done, look for the options of what can be done. Build a solution based on the resource you have. Write down everything, and everybody needed to achieve the objective. Keep working until you have an idea of what you can do to solve the problem or address the issue. Make sure you write as much as possible and record everything.

Develop and add creative skills. Some people are born creative and thrive in creative environments. Some people don't feel they have a creative bone in their body. Either way, creativity is a skill that can be taught and developed. There are a variety of different opportunities to develop creativity. They now have paint and sip, where you can combine drinking wine with painting a picture with a group. You can join an art class or go to a poetry night. You can download creative apps on your phone and create a personal logo or a flyer for a charity event. There are no limits to how you can push your creative boundaries.

The life and the world you desire to live in might not exist in your current reality, but you have the ability to create it. Inside your mind are the solutions to all your problems, a guide to your heart's desired destination, and the map to your life's treasures.

BE CREATIVE COACHING SUPPORT QUESTIONS:

BE THE GREATEST.

- HOW DO YOU EXPRESS YOUR CREATIVITY?

- WHAT NEW PROJECT CAN YOU CREATE TO STRETCH YOUR CREATIVITY?

- HOW WELL DO YOU WORK WITH OTHER CREATIVE PEOPLE? HOW DO YOU KNOW THIS?

- HOW OFTEN DO YOU BRAINSTORM DIFFERENT IDEAS BEFORE PLANNING?

THOUGHTS OF GREATNESS

BE THE GREATEST.

GREATNESS DEVELOPMENT ACTION ACTIVITIES:

BE THE GREATEST.

HELP SOMEONE ELSE WITH A PROBLEM THAT DOESN'T CONCERN YOU. LEND YOUR CREATIVE EAR TO AN EXTERNAL ISSUE.

CREATE SOMETHING NEW. START A NEW PROJECT. IT COULD BE A BOOK, STARTING A BUSINESS, GOING BACK TO SCHOOL, OR BUYING A HOUSE.

RELAUNCH A PROJECT FROM THE PAST AND FIND WAYS TO MAKE IT WORK BETTER THAN EVER BEFORE. FIND THE MISSING PIECES THAT WILL LAUNCH THE PROJECT TO NEW HEIGHTS.

THOUGHTS OF GREATNESS

Be a Visionary

Being a visionary is vital on the quest to BE THE GREATEST. Having a vision helps you stay focused and locked in on your goals. When I don't have a plan or a vision for myself, I feel lost, so I know firsthand the value of a vision. It has been proven that companies and teams that have a vital mission and vision fare better in the marketplace than those that don't. Having a solid mission is both personal and professionally beneficial. Strong missions and visions help motivate and guide you on your mission to BE THE GREATEST. When you stand in your Greatness, the people involved will also have permission to stand in their Greatness.

Personal solid leadership and focus are required to execute the mission and vision. Those who have learned to BE THE GREATEST version of themselves have the idea and what it takes to complete. A visionary can inspire a sense of purpose and inspire how allotted time is spent by being definitive about what they want to see manifested.

When I worked with the Bank, I set a goal to make a certain number of monthly sales. I knew that if I hit a certain number for the company, I would be able to reach my personal financial goal in commissions. I locked in and became a top performer. Over time I aimed for the number one spot. I was accustomed to being in the top 5 monthly. I set a goal and focused. Out of the over 1500 people from around the country, who did the same job, I had the vision to be in the top spot and developed the mindset and work ethic to get me there.

As a result of my vision to be a top performer, I was promoted to a management position. On the last day as a customer marketing associate, before I assumed my new role, I was still one of the top-performing associates in the company. When the daily report came out, I was in the spot I was used to seeing my name in, the top.

The following Monday, when I walked in to assume my new leadership role, I was assigned the lowest-performing team in the building because their manager was going to be out for a few months dealing with some personal issues. My name was at the bottom of the list when I took over the team. Very few people ever hit the minimum requirement, and none was making the available commissions for exceeding the sale quota. I was accustomed to getting a monthly commission and had never missed one.

On that day, I created a vision for that team. I didn't like seeing my name at the bottom and wanted to see people on the team get the feeling I had each month when I got my commission check. My goal was to teach each person the exact formula I used to become successful. I knew it would take time because of the different skill levels and mindsets.

The very first thing I did was call a meeting so I could share my vision with the team. I told them that each person had the potential to get a monthly commission and do more for their family and themselves if they applied the right effort. I assured them I had done it many times and knew they could. Some people believed and bought in on the spot. Others didn't see the vision and didn't believe it was possible for them. I assured them we would find a way to succeed together.

I had a team of 20 people that reported directly to me. I set aside 10 hours per week to have 30-minute one on ones with each person. I spent time talking about their vision for family and the job. We discussed what extra money could do for their family. Some people even told me they gave up on making an incentive and got an extra job.

Several people who had never made a commission got their first incentive check the first month. The team's name was no longer at the bottom of the list on the final report. The team was no longer the worst-performing team in the building. I had a vision, the group adopted it, and we achieved a goal together. Without a vision and a goal, the team would have remained at the bottom. We never became a top-performing team, but we achieved things that the team never accomplished before my arrival. The success highlighted the need for a clear vision of where you desire to be.

Years later, I had a vision for each class when I transitioned into the classroom as a high school teacher. My vision for my class was to ensure that each student had a B or higher. When students bought into the vision, they started to form habits that increased their productivity. I sold the students a vision for their future. Even though every student didn't reach the goal, my class average did. It has been proven from corporate America to the classroom that having a vision benefit all involved.

As a visionary, I learned to manage purpose and guide vision to communicate and speak beyond the day and current situation. I leveraged my optimism to create a vision of something that could be shared with all people. I witnessed my vision motivate and inspire a team and students to act and reach higher. Visionaries are a vital part of pushing our world toward Greatness.

People who lack a vision have a hard time presenting ideas and forward-thinking. A lack of vision is counterproductive when managing purpose and working toward goals. A leader who is not a visionary may leave some of the team behind and lack the patience needed for progression. These leaders often lack the day-to-day follow-up or neglect to take the appropriate steps to ensure that each person is progressing. Any person or leader who has not mastered managing vision and purpose must gather resources to help develop this area because you cannot BE THE GREATEST without a vision.

Mission and Vision Fundamental:

Get a Mission. Anyone seeking to develop a managing vision and purpose must ensure they have a mission to rally around. Companies have mission statements that they hope will capture the imagination. A clear mission will help people understand how to allocate their time and inspire more passion for consistently completing tasks. A clear mission helps build a common mindset that gives everyone a rallying point. When a visionary can clearly articulate a joint mission and vision, they can clearly show others how to add value and set a measurement for achievement.

Missions and vision are in place as motivational aids. Visions and missions are built on goals, optimism, and hope for the future. Visionaries can deliver a mission and vision with powerful and moving expressions. To inspire using mission and visions, a visionary understands the audience and the message being conveyed.

Be a Change Leader. A natural part of mastering mission and vision management is effectively dealing with resistance to change. A new mission and vision are often introduced, varying from business to usual. Many people will reject change even if it is for the best. A leader who can effectively manage vision and mission must be a change leader. A change leader can expect a certain amount of resistance, and time must be set aside to address and fix problems and issues with making changes. A change leader knows that encouragement, experimentation, and collaboration are needed to pull off organizational changes successfully.

Spearhead a project. To master being a Visionary, it is vital to be able to see a project from the beginning to the end. The project doesn't have to be a vast or professional undertaking. Create a new project for a group of friends or family. Plan a group trip for friends and family. Create a theme and find a place and time to make it happen. Get involved in planning a family reunion. Find a charity organization and get involved with a fundraiser. There are limits to what can be created when you have a vision.

BE COMPASSIONATE SUPPORT QUESTIONS:

BE THE GREATEST.

WHAT IS THE VISION YOU HAVE FOR YOUR LIFE OR BUSINESS?

HOW CAN YOU IMPROVE ON MANAGING YOUR VISION AND MISSION?

WHO IS IN YOUR VISIONARY CIRCLE? WHO DO YOU SHARE YOUR VISION WITH? DO YOU ENCOURAGE EACH OTHERS VISION? HOW CAN YOU BE MORE SUPPORTIVE?

HOW COULD YOU BE MORE EMPATHETIC WHEN DEALING WITH OTHER PEOPLE'S NEEDS AND PROBLEMS?

THOUGHTS OF GREATNESS

GREATNESS DEVELOPMENT ACTION ACTIVITIES: BE THE GREATEST.

BUILD A MASTERMIND VISIONARY ALLIANCE TO HELP ENCOURAGE AND REFINE YOUR VISION.

WORK AS A COACH OR MENTOR TO THOSE LESS EXPERIENCED AND GUIDE THEM TO THE COMPLETION OF A SUCCESSFUL PROJECT.

BE A CHANGE LEADER BY CREATING A SYMBOL OF CHANGE OR INITIATING A RALLYING CRY. IT COULD BE SOMETHING LIKE ENCOURAGING A MORE POSITIVE WORK ENVIRONMENT.

THOUGHTS OF GREATNESS

BE THE GREATEST.

Be Bold

To BE THE GREATEST, you will be required to take bold actions. There was a time when I talked about my ambitious desires, but I never took action. In today's world, many people get more gratification from posting on social media than from working to achieve their goals. It seems that many people like the way achieving something sounds but are not fond of the work required to get the task complete. They let procrastination stop the action. When striving for Greatness, you must be action-oriented when it comes to getting things done. Many successful people say that being action-oriented is a top skill. Taking timely action is a skill of Greatness that should be focused on and developed.

During my cancer battle, I made one of the boldest moves of my life when I stopped taking traditional chemotherapy for a non-traditional approach. Many people, including my loved ones and doctors, thought I was making a mistake. After dealing with the side effects of the treatment, I was ready for some bold actions as I desired an alternative approach to my cancer-fighting battle. My doctors warned me about the potential danger I was putting myself in, but I believed in my ability to beat cancer my way. Once I made up my mind, there was no turning back or doubting. Success was the only option, and nothing else was even a consideration.

The day I stopped my treatment, my doctors took some bloodwork to see where I was before going another route. My white blood count was very low, making me vulnerable to infections. I was advised that something could be added to the chemotherapy infusions to help improve some of my side effects. At this point, I didn't want any further injections. I decided to stick with my decision to go another route. Even though my insurance covered most of my medical bills, I took a chance on a process that was not covered by my insurance. I spent tens of thousands of dollars cash out of my saving account to invest in different programs, therapeutics, and remedies.

I left the cancer center in Arizona and went to a cancer healing program in Loveland, Colorado, at Eden Valley. I adjusted my mindset and took on unconventional activities to heal my mind and body. I took fever bathes in 110-degree water, spent hours in the hyperbaric oxygen chamber, adopted a vegan diet, worked out daily, and took a ton of natural medicines to help rebuild my body. I could feel my body getting stronger but had no idea if it was working. After a few weeks of intense natural treatments, I went back to my doctor for a follow-up.

When they saw my bloodwork, the doctors were all surprised at the extreme improvements. My white blood count was out of the danger zone, and my pre-diabetic status was reversed. I had also lost weight and was healthy despite still having stage 4 cancer. All four cancer spots in my body had shrunk to the point that they were not visible on the original scans. Without taking bold action, there is no way I can guarantee that I would be here with my health, life, and good spirits.

I have learned in this life that the boldest thing you can do is bet on yourself. There was a time in the middle of the biggest battle of my life when I stood alone. I had to make the best decision for me and my survival. I would have loved to have unwavering support from everyone, but that will never be the case. There will be times when you must believe in yourself and your vision. Even when other people can't see it, you must see it and be bold enough to take massive action.

People skilled at taking bold action enjoy working hard to get things done. These individuals generally enjoy setting goals and getting them done consistently. Bold people have confidence in their abilities, and they can act with minimal planning when needed. This often leads to more opportunities, and a person striving for Greatness knows just how to seize them.

A person who is unskilled at taking bold actions can easily

be identified because they are usually slow to act. Most times, the delay is because they are afraid to make mistakes, take risks, to methodical or perfectionist. People who are not bold are often masters of procrastination. They are less likely to set challenging goals and act on plans. The unskilled person usually knows what to do but doesn't have the confidence to work on it. The lack of action can lead to or result from a lack of motivation. When you hear someone say they are bored or burned out, chances are they are unskilled when taking bold action.

> You could sit back and talk about it quietly or you could speak volumes by taking massive BOLD actions and making it happen. It's all on you.

Action Based Fundamentals

Build Self Confidence. Confidence in self and ability is a must for anyone striving for Greatness and a staple of those skilled at taking bold action. People lacking in confidence can also be found to lack when taking bold action. To help build more confidence in self and ability, people can take additional courses in the lacking area, find a successful mentor, and learn from their experiences. Focusing on the strength site while developing in low areas will also help build a strong leader's confidence to take bold action.

Go for the small wins. Start small, then grow. Some actions require you to take a chance and push the envelope when trying bold new initiatives. The bigger and bolder the actions usually mean more risk and an opportunity for mistakes. Instead of going for the gusto right out of the gate, start small so that when you make an inevitable mistake, you can bounce back quickly with little or no downtime. Don't be afraid to make mistakes. Research shows that successful people make more mistakes than those who don't make them. Each error is a chance to learn and streamline the process for future endeavors. They keep working on the small wins until you are ready for the big leagues.

Get started ASAP. One of my favorite quotes says, "Procrastination is the enemy of productivity." Many people wait until the last minute and feel they work the best under pressure with deadlines approaching. The truth is that working under these terms unnecessarily undermines performance strategies. When there is a delay in the beginning, it decreases the momentum.

If people get started with projects as soon as possible, they can better gauge the time and effort needed to accomplish the task. Doing a little at a time will make significant and intimidating tasks much more manageable. By breaking big goals down into smaller ones, the likelihood of finishing them increases tremendously. The key to eliminating procrastination and becoming action-oriented is to get started immediately.

Do something BOLD today. Don't wait another day before you take advantage of the liberation to operate in your highest self. Outside of your comfort zone lies your true freedom. Be BOLD and live your Greatest Life.

BE BOLD COACHING SUPPORT QUESTIONS:

BE THE GREATEST.

WHAT CAN YOU DO TO BUILD CONFIDENCE IN YOURSELF TO TAKE BOLD ACTION?

WHAT BOLD PROJECT HAVE YOU BEEN PROCRASTINATING ON THAT YOU CAN START TODAY?

WHAT INTEREST CAN YOU RESURRECT TO INSPIRE THE PASSION NEEDED TO TAKE ACTION? WHO CAN YOU PARTNER WITH TO HOLD YOU ACCOUNTABLE FOR ACTING?

WHEN WAS THE LAST REAL RISK THAT YOU TOOK? HOW DID IT TURN OUT? WHAT DID YOU LEARN?

THOUGHTS OF GREATNESS

BE THE GREATEST.

GREATNESS DEVELOPMENT ACTION ACTIVITIES: BE THE GREATEST.

- CREATE AND LAUNCH A NEW BOLD PROJECT OR MAKE AN OUTFIT CHANGE TO MAKE A BOLD STATEMENT.

- WORK AS A COACH OR MENTOR TO THOSE LESS EXPERIENCED AND GUIDE THEM TO THE COMPLETION OF A SUCCESSFUL PROJECT.

- FIND ONE SMALL TASK THAT YOU HAVE BEEN PROCRASTINATING ON AND GET STARTED DOING SOMETHING TOWARDS ITS COMPLETION TODAY.

THOUGHTS OF GREATNESS

BE THE GREATEST.

BE THE GREATEST Bonus Resources.

At this point, you should have worked your way through the ten jewels of Greatness. There is no set time for mastery of each jewel because we are all different and shaped differently by our life experiences. I would recommend spending time doing the work to improve in each area. If the recommendations don't work for you, find a way to find something that does. Ask different questions if you don't get the correct answers to the questions you seek.

I also included some bonus resources that might be valuable in your Quest to improve yourself.

Your Greatness is your responsibility. You were created to be Great, but only you can manifest it. Now go out there and BE THE GREATEST you can be.

GREATNESS HABIT JOURNAL

DATE	TIME	START OF DAY	END OF DAY	THOUGHT OF THE DAY

Ydrate Nelson, M. Ed

The Life Balance Wheel

On your quest to BE THE GREATEST, you will need to chart a path to get from where you are to where you desire to be. You will never reach a goal that you don't set. Picture the perfect life that you have always dreamed of. You are happy and have everything in life you desire. You are satisfied with your finances, health, family, career, self-development, and relationships. Everything is right where you how you wanted it to be. Now picture those different aspects of your life as sections of a road. If the road is perfectly balanced, we can expect a smooth ride. If the road has ups and downs, we are in for a bumpy ride.

The life balance scale is a visual snapshot of the balance in your life as it is now in a visual form. Seeing your life visually makes it much easier to put it into proper perspective and context.

Looking at the scale is like looking at a map before you travel to a new city. When you look at the map, you can see where each destination is located, so don't find yourself jumping all over the place. It saves time and helps resolve problem areas efficiently.

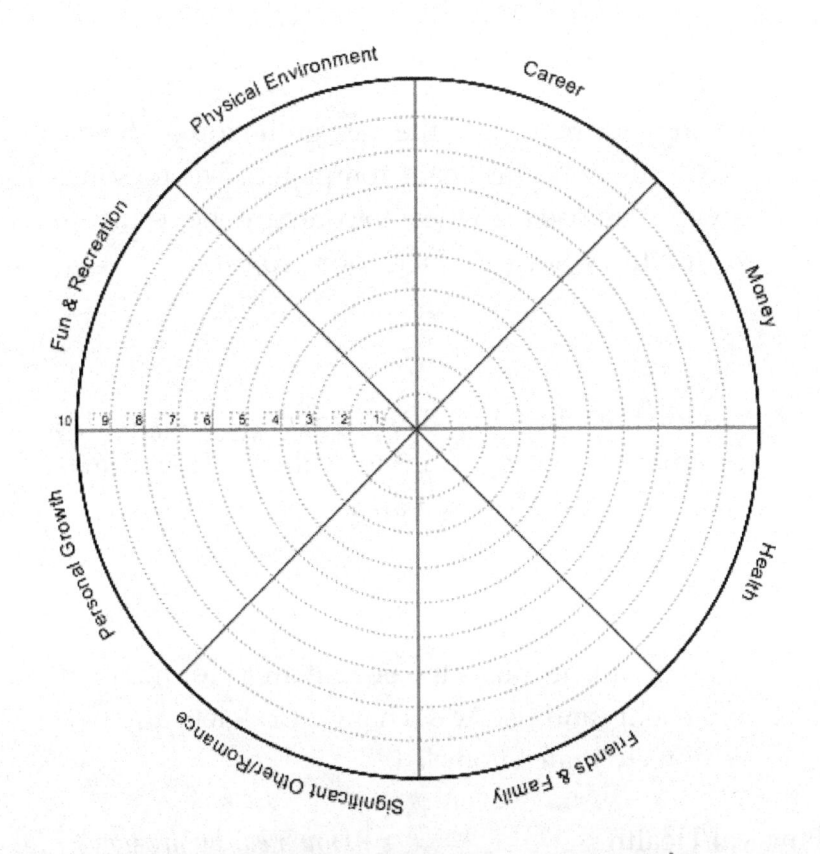

The Life Balance Wheel provided is an example of how you can draw your wheel. You can customize the areas of the wheel to match the most critical aspects of your life. Ideally, the wheel should contain 8 to 10 sections and be scaled from 1 to 10.

Let's Begin.

1. First, grab a blank piece of paper or use the section at the back of the book to draw a circle.

2. Write your name and the date at the top of the page where the wheel is being completed. The reason is so you can use the wheel to compare the results to future life wheels to track your progress.

3. Divide the wheel into 8-10 areas depending on the number of sites you want to evaluate. Then draw a score from 0-10 for each area.

4. The spreadsheet lists ten critical areas for many of my clients and us. Add, change, or delete any ten regions to match your list.

Physical/Health	*How healthy are you right now?*
Financial/Money	*How are your finances now?*
Personal Growth/development	*Do you spend time improving your mental health?*

Fun recreation	*Do you spend enough time doing the things you enjoy in life?*
Spiritual	*Are you spending time to develop spiritually?*
Romance/ intimacy	*Do you spend enough time with your partner?*
Career/Job	*Are you satisfied with your chosen career path?*
Relationships/ family, friends	*How is your family life just now?*
Motivation	*Are you satisfied with the level of internal motivation?*
Social Life and Engagement	*Are you satisfied with the level of social and life engagement?*

5. Rate each area from the wheel, chart, or by choice on a scale from 1-10. Write the first number that comes to mind. Don't spend much time on the number. Be honest with yourself, and don't overthink the results. A one doesn't necessarily

mean bad, and ten doesn't always mean good. The actual results are in the improvement and not the initial number.

6. After each area has been scored, write down the ideal score for each area. You can write your ideal score as 10 in all categories. It is important to remember that the goal is not to get all 10s but to create a more balanced life.

7. Now, look at the wheel based on where you are and want to be. This will give you a visual representation of the areas to focus on for more balance.

This exercise gets you in the mindset to think about your life and where you are now. The scale helps you look at the areas you are doing well in and where you may choose to improve. Seeing the wheel on paper will help give another perspective.

Your subconscious mind will start working on ways to improve the different areas of your life. Chances are, you already know what to do but seeing makes you more likely to act.

Remember to think about the different areas of your life daily. A daily review keeps you focused on the improvements. The goal is not to be perfect in all categories but to have balance.

We'll be discussing this more later in the program.

Recommendation: Choose one area from the chart that you want to focus on.

Answer the following questions in the journal section at the back of the book or in the provided areas.

What area do I wish to focus on? Why?

How can you improve your scoring areas?

What can you do to move this area closer to my target immediately?

What will happen when I reach the target for this area?

How will improving this area in my life impact other areas?

What other areas will be affected the most?

After you are done with one area, choose another area and repeat the questions as often as needed.

Create Mantra Statements

A mantra is a short group of positive affirmations that can be a catalyst for helping to change your life on your quest to BE THE GREATEST. A good personal mantra is an excellent way to self-motivate and affirms the life you desire to live. The words you choose have great power, and the mantras are a perfect way to create positive vibes for you and everyone you meet.

Positive thoughts and affirmations help reshape how you think about yourself and the world. Find thoughts that serve and empower you. If you do not find affirmations and positive thoughts that suit you, create your own from the inner spirit or by using the guides in this book. Your truth and answers come from within. Remember, you own your thoughts and the ability to motivate yourself.

You must choose positive and inspiring words and thoughts. The right words can push you to greatness and inspire others to reach the heights of achievement. The right positive words can change the world as you know it.

1. On the left-hand side of the chart on the following pages, list the top three things you want to change in your life. Write them in "I am" statements. For example- I am mad, I am stressed, and I am trapped. Fill them in the blanks below.

2. On the right-hand side of the chart, write the opposite of what you wrote on the left side. For example, I might be happy and blissful if I am mad.

3. String the three statements on the positive right side of the chart together to make a statement. Write the mantra in the order of your pleasing. For example, a mantra might be:

Example: *I am in a relaxed state of mind working towards everlasting peace and financial freedom.*

Recommendation: Type and handwrite your new customized mantra the way you like. Always keep a copy close. Repeat the mantra several times throughout the day aloud and to yourself.

Make a habit of reading the mantras first thing in the morning and before sleeping at night. To make it easy to remember, setting the alarm on a smartphone is a great way to help form the habit of reading the mantras daily.

Continue to use the mantras daily if it is helpful to you. Use steps 1-3 to create new and personal mantras for the different areas of your life.

Where I am now	Where I desire to be
I am_____	I am_____
I am_____	I am_____
I am_____	I am_____

Mantras can be very powerful tools to help build up confidence and inner peace. Create empowering statements that help fuel your engine to success. A few powerful words can be the catalyst needed to reach a higher level of personal and professional achievement.

Write Your Mantras

GREATNESS MINDSET PRACTICE — BE THE GREATEST.

MORNING

TODAY'S GREATNESS MANTRA:
....
....

LOOKING FORWARD TO:
....
....
....

TO MAKE TODAY GREAT, I WILL:
....
....
....

EVENING

I AM GRATEFUL FOR:
....
....

PEOPLE I APPRECIATE:
....
....
....

THREE GREAT THINGS TODAY:
....
....
....

OTHER THOUGHTS OF GREATNESS
—

GREATNESS MOMENT TO REMEMBER
—

Create a Vision Statement

You need to have a vision for the future. It is much easier to accomplish meaningful goals when you understand why you are here on Earth and when you have a clear vision. This section is designed to help articulate your vision and define your purpose to help you progress on your Greatness journey.

The first step to completing a personal vision statement is to focus on your life and what is desired. The vision is a statement that will help your progress toward your accomplishments, contributions to the world, and legacy.

- Your vision statement answers the question, *"Where do I see myself in the future? Where do I want to be?"*
- A vision statement defines the ideal desired future aspirations. The statement helps paint a clear mental picture of what you want to achieve.
- The statement is an inspiration to push you to be your best and helps define why you are doing what you do.

To help guide you through the process of creating a vision statement for your life:

1. First, Answer the following questions and Fill in the blanks below to help create a vision/purpose statement.

   POWER QUESTIONS: What is your purpose? Why are you here?

   What is your vision?

   What unique skills, talents, or abilities do you have that can be used to solve problems?

   What do people say you do well?

   What do you feel you do well?

   What would you spend your time doing if time and money were no issue?

2. Use the questions and the guide below to articulate your vision statement. Feel free to add additional sentences and record the results in the notes section at the back of the book.

   To get started, fill in the blanks below and use the example to customize your vision statement.

My vision is _____.

I am committed to _____.

I intend to _____.

Edit, revise, and rewrite the statement until it says exactly what you want.

3. Write the final revised copy in the back of this book and in your journal to make it easy to read daily.

Example of a vision statement:

My vision is to travel the Earth inspiring the world; I use intrinsic genius and leadership to deliver outstanding presentations. I intend to provide world-class speaking, training & coaching services to individuals and companies worldwide."

Living and experiencing my vision statement helps me find inner peace and joy. My hope for you is that your vision statement will do the same for you. Formulate answers to the above questions, so they flow in the best way for you. Write your vision statement. Then, listen to your heart sing with the fullness of your articulated dreams.

Make sure you write the statement as if you have already achieved the elements of the statement. Some recommend keeping your vision statement to 50 words or less. I recommend fully articulating the vision you want. Do not be limited by a word count.

Recommendation:

1. Follow the steps and customize your vision statement.

2. Write your vision statement down in multiple places, including in the notes section at the back of this book.

3. Repeat your vision statement daily and update it to reflect your progression.

Procrastination is the enemy of productivity. Do It NOW! Write your Vision Statement.

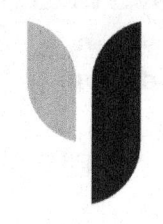

As the owner of Ydrate Nelson & Associates LLC, Ydrate specializes in Motivational Speaking, Educational Consulting, and Greatness Life Coaching.

He is a master at leveraging his cutting-edge speaking style to deliver unique keynote concerts that seamlessly fuse motivational speaking with his passion as a creative artist, to make experiences more unique, impactful, and memorable.

Ydrate is now on a mission to help others cultivate a motivated mindset for success and BE THE GREATEST version of themselves. Ydrate collaborates with students, fellow educators, entrepreneurs, and working professionals to develop the mindset, motivation, and leadership strategies to maximize their personal Greatness.

Ydrate is the creator of BE THE GREATEST U whose mission is to leverage education, fashion, influence, and entertainment to inspire higher achievement, increase self-esteem and maximize personal Greatness.

BE THE GREATEST.
Publishing

For your organization's speaking, training, and coaching need, contact Ydrate Nelson & Associates LLC. We look forward to connecting with you soon.

YDRATENELSON.COM